COVID
COMMUNITY
& COCKTAILS

COVID
COMMUNITY
& COCKTAILS

the bright side of dark times

L.A. WALKER

A MULTIMEDIA PUBLISHING COMPANY

Speaking in Volumes
12656 Southern Highlands Pkwy
Unit 1012
Las Vegas, Nevada 89141

Copyright © 2022 Social Issues Theatre
ISBN 978-1-956070-08-8
Printed by: OPA Media LLC, Las Vegas, Nevada
First printing edition 2022

CONTENTS

DEDICATION

We dedicate this series to those who, despite their challenges, have devoted themselves to demonstrating care and concern for others, to everyone who said a final goodbye to a family member, loved one, friend, or coworker during this COVID era.

We dedicate this series to all health care workers, first responders, educators, every business owner who did all to keep their employees working, and to every parent who struggled with technology and maintained a positive appearance for their children.

We dedicate this series to every politician who stayed engaged with their communities, every church and charitable organization, and everyone in the entertainment industry who placed their health in harm's way to keep us uplifted.

Thank you for bringing light to a dark time.

ACKNOWLEDGMENTS

A special thanks to Russ White, Tyler Rhea, Stacy Young, Esther Britt, Craig Young, Kyle Khou, Garrett Pattiani, and Margo Kuykendall for your heartfelt stories and interviews. Thank my supportive friend and advisor Niya Rivera, who always lets me think I'm in charge. Thanks to Social Issues Theatre's Co-Executive Director Marcia Norris, who can see a better approach to most anything, and Director of Communications Chuck Stutz for his subtle but exacting corrections. Cassie Trujillo, and Aris Lazarou, Schulman Properties, for ensuring I dotted every "I" and crossed every "T." Thank you, Winnie Schulman and Steven Kennedy Axum Hospitality, for spilling the "tea." Thank you, educator Angie Pohlman for being my personal word usage scientist.

A special thanks to the Universe for this assignment

INTRODUCTION

"COVID Community and Cocktails"

Residents reflect how living real estate developer Robert Schulman's dream to build a community with onsite dining will always be remembered as a bright spot in a dark time.

While much of the world struggled to find safe ways to engage with coworkers, and family members, buying groceries and other necessities, residents of the Tuscan Highlands apartment community found comfort sharing time with other residents over food and beverage at Becca's the onsite restaurant and sports lounge

Their shared stories tell how the deliberately designed apartment development with sensible amenities allowed a community to exist and grow during one of the darkest times in history.

The COVID and Community series is the creation of L.A. Walker, Executive Director of Social Issues Theatre for the 501c3 nonprofit's Mental Wellness and Community Unity effort.

Thank You
SOCIAL ISSUES THEATRE
SIT

bringing society together one line at a time

MENTAL WELLNESS AND COMMUNITY UNITY

Can we have an open, honest, hiding-no-truths conversation? A conversation where we will make zero apologies for stating how we feel? I hope you said yes.

These past few years have been the craziest times the world has faced together. While we were reeling from a viral pandemic, social pandemics seemed to crop up everywhere, and fear of sickness and death rested on the minds of most. Mandated business and school shutdowns birthed uncertainty about the future of the economy, education, recreation, entertainment, and family gatherings.

As we mature, we become accustomed to facing challenges, just not this many simultaneously. These last few years have saddled us with a variety of problems and have assisted many in riding off the grid, unable to cope with its stress. Reports state that depressive disorders, suicide, divorce, violence, and drug abuse have increased.

We are now entering the residual effects of the pandemic. What do we need to do? How do we encourage and uplift ourselves and others? How do we feed our need for hope and faith? Through stories, testimonies, and the sharing of multiple accounts of acts of kindness.

We must add more positivity and inspiration to balance the see-saw.

I had the fortune of speaking with real estate developer Bob Schulman. Our backdrop was a beautifully decorated wine garden, a setting on a property he created. I was hoping he didn't catch me staring at him. I intended to remember every detail about him, his facial expressions, posture, and words. Bob Schulman is a very charming man. I was seated on his left. His beautiful wife and business partner Winnie and I were facing each other. This allowed me to observe their expressions as they spoke passionately about how and why building a place that would encourage community was so important to them. As they talked, I began to understand why every employee in every department presented genuine pleasantness, politeness, and kindness. Their love for people and their combined desire to promote goodwill, diversity, and inclusiveness is married to their passion for beauty and comfort. They wanted residents to enjoy living every day. They injected their energy into every facet of the property.

RUSS WHITE

Entrepreneur
Technologist
Publisher

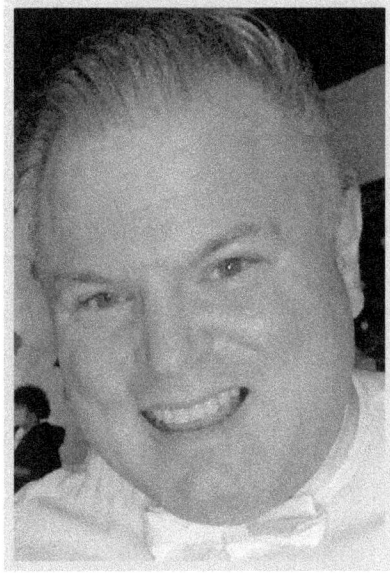

In the wake of 9/11, I had to sell my home. I had a high Silicon Valley mortgage, no job, no job market, and a stock portfolio that was quickly evaporating. I moved into a new mid-rise apartment complex—one of the first new residents in the community. As others started moving in, I made friends with neighbors. I quickly realized that there were others without jobs. Others without prospects. Others without wealth or rapidly dissipating wealth. While we were West Coast, we lived in the aftermath of 9/11 together. The following weeks would bring spontaneous barbecues by the pool, late nights in the hot tub, pool parties mid-day, working out together, and sharing our homes. The events of 9/11 occurred in New York and Washington, D.C. Yet, the repercussions were global and beyond comprehension for those not directly affected. However, 9/11 brought a community together in the aftermath and created lifelong friendships that I hold dear to this day.

Fast forward to 2020. A global event unfolded before us. An even more massive scale impact that somehow affected nearly everyone on the planet. I was living in a high-rise on the Las Vegas Strip. I had fulfilled my dream of living among the neon lights. I suddenly found myself without an income. All my clients canceled. My landlord decided to sell my home with no income. I would have to find a new place to live.

I received a postcard in the mail for a brand-new apartment community. I went to check things out. Even though the property was still under construction, I saw the vision and potential and signed right away. I was one of the first to move into the community. Things were starting to feel repetitive—a global crisis. No job. New apartment. New community. Things are different when you move into a new community. As new neighbors moved in, it was inevitable that we would get to know one another. The state had shut down, so we couldn't go many places.

One of the most significant attractions of this apartment community was the onsite bar and restaurant. Becca's was our saving grace. Taco Tuesdays, Friday night mixers, and Sunday brunch became part of our lives in the middle of the pandemic. People came together, contributing to spontaneous uplifting gatherings. We created a bubble around our amenities during the pandemic while others were left without any options.

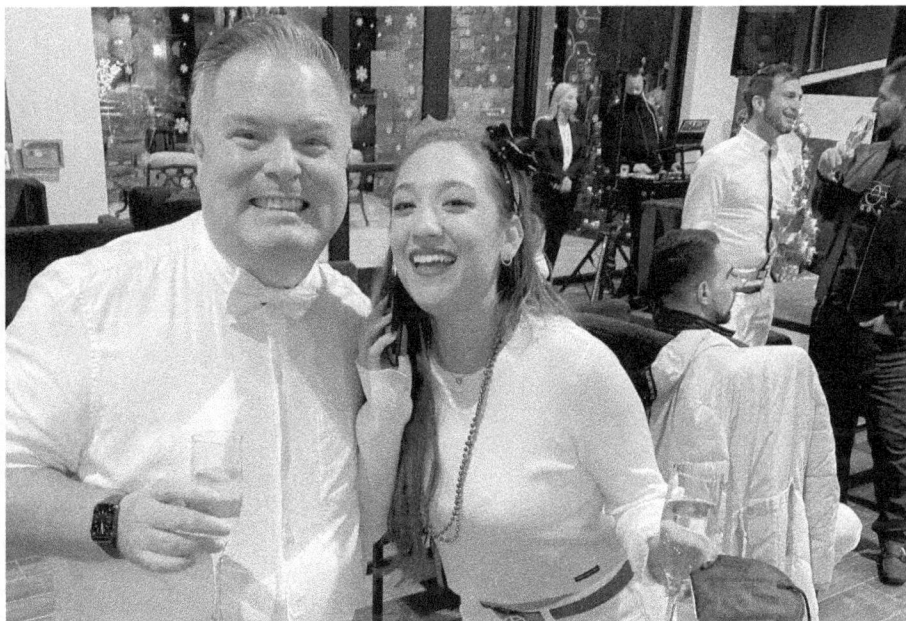

TYLER RHEA

Renewable Engineering Consultant

AMBIVERT:/ambe, vert/
It is a Psychological term that depicts a person whose personality has a balance of extrovert and introvert features.

Like many people, I don't fit into one single defiance category. I like to be extremely social, communal, and even gregarious. On the flip side, I like to be home alone where I can be well, just be. Watch whatever I want to watch, eat whatever I want to eat. I can listen to my music that most would find bazaar without judgment or opinions. That's why I feel resort living has helped me find a healthy balance of both sides of myself because I can do both at any given the time of day.

▌THE YEAR THAT WAS 2020

After coming off of a Rocky two years (i.e., 2018,2019), I was excited to usher in a new decade with new goals and excitement like everyone else in the world. However, the world had a different plan to help us welcome the new decade with a global crisis and a racial pandemic all rolled into the same year. At the top of the year, I had just gotten a new position in the company I am with and was working like crazy.

I can't even recall the many times I said I wish I could take a couple of months off to do absolutely nothing. Not talk to anyone, not have any responsibilities, not have to work. Just a couple of months to sit around and do nothing. As I'm sure most people have thought the same thing at some point in their life, 2020 would prove to get that wish granted for everyone across the world. While most were worried about health and dying, I was the opposite. I was excited to be quarantined. I had been planning this for years! My true introvert was about to take over to the full extent.

Before the shutdown, I prepared not to be scared in my house but to enjoy it! I did what everyone else did. I rushed to the grocery store-bought a bunch of unhealthy food to cook. I wanted to work on my culinary skills. I filled up the tank and even hired a house cleaner to clean the entire house so I didn't have to. I wanted no responsibilities at all! The first day I woke up super late because I didn't have to go to work yup that's right, I slept until 6:05 am instead of waking up at my normal time at 6:00 am. I woke up, took a shower, got dressed, and headed to Starbucks. I know I could wait to bring home my Venti Chai tea latte with four pumps of cinnamon dolce, no water, oat milk, extra hot at 190 degrees, add whip cream on top with caramel drizzle on top of the whip and cinnamon dolce power as a topper. Yes, that is the Starbucks drink I've been ordering for the past 11 years. You would have thought my name was Becky or Suzanne, but it's so good! I couldn't wait now more than ever to have that piping hot tea and come home and watch something on HBO MAX,

which had just launched that same week. Only to find out Starbucks was closed. I had forgotten we are in quarantine. I wondered why the streets were empty and why there was no Honda Odyssey in the line at 7:30 in the morning. That would prove to be the case for the next three months. I did have my subscriptions, though; I cleared out most of all my watchlists, connected with old friends and families over the phone, and even got back into gaming. If you know anything about gaming, you know that to play GRAND THEFT AUTO V Online takes a minute to level up. I played online with my family, and I went from level 1 to 228 in 3 months! That's a lot of hours logged in to gaming. All of which could have been used for a better purpose. By mid-April, I couldn't help but wonder when this crisis would be over. I began to want to go outside again and go out to a restaurant, a cafe, a hookah lounge, a club, and, most importantly, a Movie theater. I could do none of that. My extrovert side was getting restless. I started sleeping until 10 am and, going to bed at 3 am, ate at all times of the day with no thought of numerical value. Meanwhile, I'm watching my peers workout from home, getting in the best shape of their life to become only fans models. I was beginning to realize I miss socializing. I miss being around people and laughing and creating memories. May had crept around quickly, and all I wanted to do was travel. I wanted to go back to Italy or go to the Dominican Republic or Ghana, or anywhere where there was sun and water. Little did I know in that same month, on May 25th, I would witness a video that sparked a global outrage of yet another senseless killing of an unarmed black man. George Floyd's murder ignited the furry in me to say to hell with the health codes. It's time to take action. Peacefully protesting and silently helping in my community to make things right would be the task I needed to help me be social again. After being on lockdown for so long, the slightest bit of contact with another human is very refreshing. I wondered about my old complex that I lived in, "SOUTH BEACH." A resort-style living environment placed people together outside of a work element to interact and make new friends. I was missing that. As I had moved due to a shift in my life in 2018 that would see my relinquishing lease there. I set out to go back there, but only if I had the same Unit where I once lived. As I tried my best to get back into that Unit, it would be an exercise in futility. The Unit I wanted became available, but South Beach rented that one despite me being on the waitlist for it. To say I was devastated was an understatement. But everything happens for a reason, and everything that has a beginning has an end. When one story ends, the other picks up. A couple of weeks later, I would get a text from Winnie Schulman, the owner of South Beach, informing me that the second property she was working on was nearing completion. Not a second went by before I got dressed and headed up to the construction site. This was it. It was what I wanted to relive again a secluded complex that had social amenities to allow people to converse and create new relationships. Now let's be clear here, I have no problem making friends or being social. There are times when I want to be alone at home, and at any given moment, I can bounce up and say I'm bored and want to do something. Or on the other hand, I am in a social mood, and at any given time, I can say "I'm Over It" and go home immediately. This property allows that. It allows me to go out without worrying about making plans with others and being committal if I don't want to be. I'm the type of guy who will be excited all week to go out with the homies and then get a text saying, "so and so can't make it let's reschedule" SAY LESS! I go back into sweat pants, order a pizza and watch a movie on my big screen or play PS5. Along the way, I have been fortunate to meet certain people that I consider more than just neighbors; I consider them friends now. We went to the movies every week, coming up with group costumes to wear to a Halloween party (Which, by the way, we won as if there was any competition, to begin with.) Going out to dinner on a random night, celebrating each other's birthdays and accomplishments, and truly being happy for them. Where most people are still alone because of COVID and not being able to go out, or the only "friends" they make is at work, this community can break down that wall and help them be social again. 2020 and 2021 have been great years, and I am looking forward to 2022 traveling the world and making new connections, friendships, and relationships. My advice during these times is to let these moments push you to improve yourself in all areas of your life. At work, at home, activism, spirituality, wherever you can find hope and peace. Follow It and remember you are never alone. Lean on that strength of togetherness, keep the collective strength, and stay focused. Don't talk about what you're going to do, don't just dream about what you want to do, don't criticize someone else for what they are doing, be about it, be about that action, and do it. Don't let any outside distractions or insecurities stop you from your goals or purpose. There will be many failed attempts. Trust me, I know. I have been saying since January 2021 that I was going to get into shape and go to the gym consistently. It is hard, but I try now and then and go, but it has not been consistent. I fail too, but one day I won't! That struggle will strengthen you. My prayer for anyone is to invest in yourself and see the power within yourself to give the best life to yourself that you can. Read that sentence again, and it will make sense to you. Celebrate and value your life and all lives. Everyone is beautiful. Your blackness is beautiful. Your queerness. Your wideness or Whiteness is beautiful when you are in a room full of others who don't look like you, sound like you, talk like you, dress like you, or maybe not even like you because you don't look or act like them. Remember, you're beautiful in your way. I say all that to say is if COVID didn't teach us anything, it taught us to live! We could no longer be here at any moment and any day. Live, be happy, be social, be YOU!

ESTHER BRITT

Educator

CRAIG YOUNG

Account Clerk
the City of
Guadalupe

STACY YOUNG

Attorney

Stacy Young, Esther Britt, and Craig Young three residents tell of their shared experience living through COVID-19 is uplifting and serves as a reminder of the power of community to create hours of joy amid world sadness.

Rarely is COVID-19 associated with bright days and fun times.

L.A. Walker

Where did you move from?

Stacy Young

Herriman Utah!

L.A.

How did Herriman, Utah, residents respond to COVID-19?

Stacy

Um, we had lots of fear. Fear, you know, that this disease would kill everybody at first. And so we had to socially distance and wear masks.

I was a classroom school teacher for several years. Suddenly, due to the presence of COVID-19, I had to learn how to teach online, which was new to me. I was the teacher, and I taught in person, and I never had any training for teaching online. I did introduce myself to use the online platforms, you know, to reach kids. I had to do full in-person and online classes for the kids out for sickness or quarantine because they had someone they knew had been sick. And so it was a lot of work, a lot.

And then that last year, I taught with masks. And that was on the heels of not going to school, you know, so the kids were excited to be back. The students loved being back, and we were in masks all year.

L.A.

What made you move to Las Vegas?

Stacy

Um, it was weather and retirement. I left my teaching job. My husband Craig had sold his law practice. And so we had the freedom to choose where we wanted to live. So we came to Las Vegas. I was tired of snow, and we had a lot of snow in Utah. And, and we also liked Las Vegas, we like the people, we like the diversity. We appreciate all of the offerings that Las Vegas has as far as entertainment and just a variety that we didn't have back in Harriman. It was great to come here and remove masks, talk to people, and see their faces.

L.A.

What has been your most enormous surprise since moving?

Stacy

I would say the sense of community is a surprisingly pleasant surprise. Because the great thing about I think being here is you get a diversity of backgrounds of ethnicities of cultures, but everyone seems to accept the other where they are or whatever their viewpoints. So, for instance, some people wanted to wear masks and others didn't, but it didn't become this big polarizing problem here. It seemed like everyone accepted the other for where they were. Also, the unique thing about the complex was it seemed to, for an apartment community, give us a sense of looking out for our neighbor. If you didn't see someone you know, you would inquire. Esther's not in yoga today. You or a neighbor would call. Esther, are you okay? Do you need some food or anything? She would look in on us, and we looked in on other neighbors, which was a pleasant surprise.

There are plenty of lovely, secluded apartments, but this complex allows you to be yourself at your comfort level.

L.A. Walker

Esther, where are you from, and what brought you to Las Vegas?

Esther Britt

I am originally from New York, New York. I lived there for about 27 years and moved to California. I was there for almost 30 years. And then I came out to Las Vegas. The reason for my leaving California, my daughter moved from California to Las Vegas. So Las Vegas was not my first choice, but when my daughter moved, I wanted to be around my grandson, which brought me to Vegas, and I'm so grateful that I am here.

L.A.

How does living in this community differ from your other living experiences?

Esther

The part that differentiated itself from other apartment complexes with pools and barbecues was that they also had specific classes on specific days and times. So you could go with your neighbors and participate in activities of common interest. And I remember Stacy's eyes lit up when we saw they had a calendar of classes. So we didn't have to join a separate gym. You know, it's not an extra added charge. And it's like, Oh, that's nice. And so, I think it was the classes, but also the restaurant. The food provides that opportunity to get together and share a meal and share some stories.

My family members ask me if I live in a 55+ Senior Retirement Community, and I tell them no. And they reply, "I never heard of a place that feeds you three times a week and gives you access to classes without charging an extra fee." It's in our lifestyle plan, and we pay, but not what it would cost us on the outside. First, everything is at your fingertips. You don't have to drive, and you don't have to spend extra money on everything. I love it. I feel safe.

L.A. Walker

You left a city of approximately 55,000 residents where you enjoyed the comfort of knowing your neighbors. Did you have any apprehension about moving to a new development in Las Vegas?

Craig Young

I want to say how easy it's been to make friends here. Because everybody's relatively new no one's been here 10 or 20 years. It hasn't been around very long. So we're all new, and we're all open to meeting new people and meeting new friends. And it doesn't matter your age, race, or origin. We have met and know international people. We have international friends now that will be lifelong friends and people of all ages, colors, and sizes. And we love that so much because we came from a more homogenous area. And so we appreciate how everybody accepts everybody, wherever you're at, and there's like, it doesn't matter what politics you have, what religion you have, or however your family looks. It's significantly come as you are. Residents and staff accept where you are, wherever you are right now. And that's been so enjoyable for us.

L.A.

Craig, why do you think residents were successful as a community in surviving the 2020-2022 viral, racial, political, and gender pandemics? What made setting aside those polarizing topics or aspects of life possible?

Craig

I think we came together and saw similarities more than differences. And we saw Oh, we all enjoy this yoga class. And that's why we're all together in this yoga class. And, and so it's easy to make friends in yoga class, or we all enjoy coming back together and enjoying a meal together. And so we saw the similarities instead of the differences because you can see that with anybody. It is your choice whether you see the similarities or the differences, and we are all choosing to see the similarities.

L.A.

How did the presence of Becca's Restaurant and Lounge assist in bolstering community unity?

Craig

What do you feel when you think of restaurants? You think great food. You think alcohol, and you think relaxation, you think socialization. We experienced all of that at Becca's, and I also think all the candy around us helped us. When you go to the pool, you feel the same thing. You go to the classes, and you think the same thing? The ritual of being together meant that I did not want to be separated from you. You know, it's just very, very welcoming.

Perspective, so I think that purpose and intent have everything to do with the outcome of life. So the builder's greatest desire to build something that would bring people together laid out the foundation, but the application was still up to us. We walked in, and we wanted that to happen. And we wanted it to happen at a time when we desperately needed it to happen.

Stacy

Absolutely. Yes.

Craig

We're social creatures, not meant to live as hermits, isolated from the world. And so when we had to be for a while, it helped us slow down and value and re-evaluate what makes us human and makes us, you know, better people.

Stacy

Absolutely. I also have to say that meeting some of the people who work here, like I enjoy Stephanie and Matt and their work to help us have these good times. And also, Terrell is our next-door neighbor. He's the groundskeeper here, and he is so wonderful. He is fantastic!

Terrell always smiles. We are so appreciative of all the hard work he does here. And the staff at the restaurant. The bartenders do a great job. The class instructors in the gym bring positivity, and we benefit from that. We feel it, and it rubs off on us. And we've experienced this positive energy our entire time here. There was someone else I wanted to mention. Andrea, in the leasing office, we felt it from her right away when we moved in. And so we talked with her, and she said, I live here too. And we're like, wow, because usually, the person working at the desk doesn't live on the property, and the groundskeeper doesn't live on the property, but we all live here together.

Esther

The coaches like Tess, and Susie, I look forward to going to their classes because I am doing my exercise, but I also have fun while I'm doing it. I've never worked out in my life. My son says, Mom, I'm so proud of you.

Just keep it up. Before I moved, my son was nervous about me moving to Las Vegas. "You don't know anybody there," he said. And when he came, and we sat by the pool, he said, "this is nice." But the second time he came to visit, he said, " mom, I feel pretty safe." I said you do? And he said "yes." He said the people are really friendly.

L.A.

Stacy, Esther, and Craig thank you for sharing. Your stories are warm and joyously inspiring.

Vice-President Axum Hospitality Owner of Element Hospitality Partner in Becca's Restaurant, Players Locker. Beer Park & Chateau

L.A. Walker

How many adjustments did your team make to keep the restaurant open to residents during the demanding high COVID months?

Steven Kennedy

Phew! It's been a challenging two years. We followed everything from the CDC guidelines and the health department. You want to protect people and citizens in the community simultaneously, and you're trying to run a business, stay open, and make it viable. You're navigating around employees and their health and wellness and safety.

So it was, you know, from the very beginning, the rules were six outside dining, at a portion takeout only, curbside pickup, people were locked in their houses, and everybody was going on long walks to kill time.

We navigated through that. The next phase was outdoor dining, with six feet of social distancing. Those were challenging opening hours to make it worth someone's time to return to work.

When we first opened Becca's, I cooked, ran food, waited tables, and bartended. It was a growing experience as a restaurant operator, but we slowly returned to indoor dining with social distancing. We're blessed with this 10,000-square-foot patio. We designed a COVID secure buffet line with safety glass. You go to your traditional buffet, and everyone's touching the same handles, the same food, grabbing desserts.

L.A.

You know Steven, the old way no longer sounds appealing. Throughout the years, many have expressed concern about public access to food.

Steven

Yes, I agree. Coming out of the worst part of COVID, it made everybody in the business world a little bit better as an operator. It made people managing casino eateries more efficient and more concerned about cleanliness. The one thing Vegas does have over where I've consulted in other cities is probably the Health Department's strict Code of Conduct.

As an operator, you hate it when the health department comes to your door, but for the community, it's positive. Most customers don't know that grade on the window is essential, and you don't want to see a D or C grade or a dirty dining tag. I think COVID brought more uncleanliness to light, a reminder about the importance of sanitation and how to get rid of germs and all those kinds of things.

We opened in the middle of the pandemic. We didn't qualify for any government assistance, no PPP loans, or anything like that. So we were handcuffed. It was a blessing that we weren't paying fifty to sixty thousand dollars a month in rent on the strip.

As you know, many businesses didn't make it through COVID, even with the support. We were fortunate to be able to survive.. We have support from the people who live here. The local community came down and supported our business because they got a chance to go out again and eat and feel the energy and kindness of people for a while. You had a few people that didn't understand the challenges we as an operator were doing all to overcome. A few got upset when something wasn't perfect, but it was, as you know, hard sourcing food and alcoholic beverages, and it was hard sourcing labor. "Out of alcoholic alcohol? How does a bar run on alcohol?"

L.A.

Out of alcohol? How does a bar run out of alcohol? Steven, you know that was the running joke.

Steven

For anything coming over from overseas, especially France, where many of your cognacs, wines, and champagnes, are produced, most bars couldn't get them. It was hard to get glassware and different things. So during one week, you have one shape class, the next week was something different. Most of the people were amazing, and the customers were patient and just happy to be able to go out again. And then you'd have the few people that were, you know, didn't just

didn't understand the kind of challenges, but for the most part, it was quite the experience going through it all.

L.A.

So how long have you been in the restaurant bar business?

Steven

I worked part-time when I got out of college. I worked as a bar manager in Boston, plus doing finance nine to five. So I would work three nights a week. Unfortunately, living in the city and making thirty-five to forty thousand a year out of college sounded good, but it was not a sustainable lifestyle. So, I worked three nights a week at a local bar and the Financial District in Boston, and I started a business. Then I moved to California to take a job. On September 7th, I moved into my apartment in California. September 11th happened. They asked me to come back to Boston. So, I picked up the Yellow Pages and started calling around things I knew how to do, which were bartending a little bit and being a baseball player all through college. So I coached at a private baseball school, and I got into being a corporate director, opening some restaurants in California. For about a year before I came out to Vegas, I got an opportunity to manage a place here. That's been almost 21 years, I guess.

L.A.

That's amazing. Do you think your prior experiences prepared you to navigate through the pandemic?

Steven

Yeah, the experience helped, but honestly, most ran operations by the seat of our pants.

L.A.

Could you tell me one attribute you possess that contributed to your team's success?

Steven

Adaptability. I think just adapting is the key because it's not over.

L.A.

Give me an example

Steven

I think just being able to adapt and be open to working with whatever guidelines the CDC requires. That was a little frustrating. Because some of the CDC's rules were probably not made by anyone from the hospitality industry. They probably should have hired some people with twenty to thirty years of experience to help out the CDC. We would have had a smoother transition if the transition had been better thought out.

L.A.

What's your most significant takeaway from this COVID experience?

Steven

Slow down a little bit. No matter the circumstance, make sure you're enjoying yourself. Hospitality is about service, taking care of people, and appreciating multiple personalities and diversities. I think I got to re-engage back with our customers and become friends, and this experience has given me a greater appreciation for the people around me.

L.A.

That's awesome. Is there anything particular that you'd like to share?

Steven

Here we are at the two-year mark. It seems like a lifetime ago, and I don't think most understand how scary it was for casino operators. Some casino operators were like we don't have locks on our doors because they're open twenty-four hours. They were in a panic. The Las Vegas Strip without lights was a terrifying time for Las Vegas residents. I'm glad we're getting somewhat back to normal.

L.A. and Steven

We'll see.

KYLE KHOU

American Idol Casting
Producer American
Idol Season 11 Alumnus
Brown's Gymnastics
Head Coach Singer/
actor/gymnast

L.A. Walker

I remember the first night we met. Looking back is the fun part of this whole thing, realizing that I didn't know who you were. It wasn't like, oh, I met this guy, and he was an American Idol contestant. You presented yourself as simply another nice, warm, and ingratiating guy, which was why I thought, okay, I gotta move here. I can do this.

Kyle Khou

I feel the same way. It was an extraordinary first meeting. I remember driving home thinking, she's so cool. You're just so cool. I remember exactly where you were sitting in the wine garden like it happened yesterday.

L.A.

So tell me, how did you actually decide to move?

Kyle

Well, it started when I was moving to another community. An agent said, Hey, I just got onto a project. It's a couple of years out. She gave me all the details. I told myself there's no way they would make a place like that. And if there is, there's no way

I'm going to drive down there and pay for that. It looked fantastic. Too good to be true. My interest peaked. And then, she encouraged me to come down to the wine mixer. There's a mixer? Cheers. And that's where I met you. There was nothing built. There was just a front office and the wine garden, and I met you, and I met a couple of other people. And everyone was doing something extraordinary with their lives, essential things in my mind. Every job is important, but you guys felt you were changing people's lives. And I was like, this is a community I want to be a part of. I haven't seen my unit yet. But when I left, I was like, I have to be here. Because my husband was getting deployed., and I know I'm gonna be by myself. From just meeting you, Amy and Jack, and Garrett, I thought I had to live here. That was the start of a beautiful time.

L.A.

It was a fantastic time. We met in August. When did you move in? September?

Kyle

Yes, I did. So I guess we all did. I was among the first 15 people so were you. The pool wasn't open, and the restaurant wasn't open. All we had was each other and the wine garden. And that was under construction.

L.A.

Yes, I remember walking to go take a look at the units. And we were walking on wood, and they had placed planks so we wouldn't fall into the gravel. We toured the units in groups, and we bonded every step of the way. It was just fun.

In my conversations with Winnie, she shared that Bob decided to have those wine mixers against her advice, despite his advisors, and against all pessimistic probability forecasts. Because realistically, it was terrifying because the construction of the wine garden was incomplete. There could have been problems, big problems. But Bob decided that it had to happen. His intuition led him to believe that the magic was in the people gathering. They had to feel each other. They had to want to live, work, and play together.

So what was going on in your life? That was high COVID time?

Kyle

Yes, it still was during high COVID time. It was 2020, that's right. Oh my goodness. I was in a 4000 square foot house my roommate had moved out. I was just chilling and really lonely. I was like, I can't do this. I am one of 17 kids. So I grew up with people always around. I grew up with a support system always. And then I found myself in an echo at home by myself. Being out here in Vegas by myself. I have no family. I'm here. How do I go from 17 siblings to being married to being by myself? I really needed somewhere during the pandemic. I was literally going to be by myself for a whole year. I know other people are by themselves. It was a culture

shock. No dog, no animals, and no people? It was too much.

My work was shut down. I have two jobs. So, my gymnastics program was shut down. I had to work most of the day there because we only had a certain number of people in the building. There were only 20 people in the gym that prior had 600. We had to find a way to do an hour and a half to two-hour practices with each team group when there used to be four and a half to five hours a day. Other states were still open and therefore getting the benefit of their full practice time. We had to get ready for our competition season under those circumstances. I just got back to work. We weren't doing anything between March and August, and then my whole life shut down. Like everyone else's right. Athletics were shut down. Film Production was shut down. So my other job, if anyone was there, it was like you're a makeup artist? Great! You had to be a makeup artist, stylist, and film assistant. They made one person do three or four jobs to keep everything limited. So eventually, they stuck us in our homes and made us work from a computer screen.

L.A.

So you were working with American Idol?

Kyle

Yes, I was working from my living room. Want to try and learn how to cast and get to know people from the screen instead of immersive film? We had to learn a new way of trying to feel someone's energy through a computer screen, which is very difficult.

L.A.

I feel bad knowing you were met with these challenges, but I'm sure you were the guy for the task.

Kyle

Thank you. Many people missed out on opportunities because their Wi-Fi wasn't good, and they were so depressed about COVID or didn't know how to talk to a screen. But I did feel disconnected from people entirely, and I felt disconnected from my family, except for this community. It was amazing to be in this community and meet new people.

L.A.

So when did American Idol actually get back to normal? What we once considered normal.

Kyle

It's been a couple of seasons since 2020 shut down, and we're still doing stuff from our living room. We have live audiences now and during the live shows, but my work is done after the whole show is cast. So I don't think it will go back to normal. I don't think the film industry will return to what it once was. I believe they are saving so much money now. And I think a lot of companies figured out that people don't have to be stuck in the office building. The technology is so good that you can be out by the pool and still do your work. We're evolving, and I don't think it's terrible.

L.A.

How was living here a more incredible experience than other places you've lived?

Kyle

This is so cliche, but it's hard to explain if you haven't lived here and haven't been involved in it, you might not get it. I just remember a drive going to park my car, getting out of the car, and thinking, this is just a paradise. It was like being at a hotel or in Hawaii or some situation like that, but then it's also home simultaneously. So I can feel like I'm on vacation or feel at home, but it is still five stars. So if I wanted to have a vacation with you or other people or to have a vacation and a cabana by myself, I could.

But even when I walk back in here, I still like reminiscing on the magic that it was when this all came down. Bob and Winnie did such a great job with this property. The people. The people we all shared so many stories with each other. We all bonded with each other. We all went out together. I could have texted anybody and said I'm going through a hard time, let's go meet outside and immediately they'd be outside, and we just talked about everything, then we'd have a drink and go our separate ways. You can't find that anywhere. I've lived and traveled with touring groups, I've traveled with T.V. shows with gymnastics, and I've never felt an actual family away from family like this is. I don't know if this feeling can be recreated.

L.A.

In speaking with Winnie and Bob, they were vacationing in Tuscany when he turned to Winnie and said, "I need to create this so that working people can enjoy this beauty every day and not have to wait for a year; to go on vacation."

Kyle

Well, he did that. They did that. This...is that.

L.A.

The stressful presence of COVID tested every amenity, every employee, every resident, and even Bob and Winnie's faith was tested. COVID tested us all.

Kyle

I saw people light up when we saw each other every day. Every day, we walked by each other, even if it was just like, an hour before, it was hi. We just saw each other, but we were still happy to see each other. And then you would see this Goddess of a human, Winnie, walking around. Winnie is my idol. She's so calm, always pleasant and welcoming. I've been around many incredible people in my life, but this is interesting sitting here just remembering those times. Honestly, it was some of the best. It was one of the best years of my life when it came to finding myself. I feel like every several years, you have to reevaluate yourself. Living here could not have come at a better time. Something extraordinary occurred here. I moved here a week after Jameson got deployed. So it literally could not have been a better time.

L.A.

It was also the best time for me because my spouse passed away in June 2020. Honestly, I don't think I would have made it if I had not come here. When I got here, I was in so much emotional pain, and I was afraid to awaken. I felt so alone, and then I had an instant family that consisted of many nationalities, age groups, and professions. You know, it's just been so healing for me.

When did Jameson come home a year later?

Kyle

He came home about ten months later. To set this answer upright, Jameson had only visited during a wine mixer, and he didn't see our unit or get to feel the aura we lived under.

L.A.

What was his impression?

Kyle

Believe it or not, it caused a little bit of conflict when he was on deployment because he didn't understand what this place was. He got here on the weekend. I'd just be walking to the bar to get something, and then suddenly, it's an all-nighter. But he didn't get that. He was like, I thought you were just walking down to get food. I'm uh, you can't walk down and get food and come right back because it's a family. It took him a minute. He finally got it and fell in love with the magic.

L.A.

I saw the joy in him, and it was a beautiful thing to see. If I were to rewrite this whole story and fictionalize it for the big screen, I would say we were hand-picked by the universe to be here.

Kyle

I agree. I agree. Nothing should have worked out for this. I was in the middle of a lease, and the agency messed something up. So I was able to get out of the lease to be here. It shouldn't have worked out. And if I hadn't come to that wine mixer and met everybody, I don't know what direction my life would have been. I can't describe it other than it's just what I needed. Even the staff at the time. Everything was what I needed. Everything. Because I felt like I was drowning in COVID. Everything came to a stop. I needed to figure things out and listen to myself because I was just going and didn't take care of myself. I got super skinny. I felt I needed a break. I needed to realize whether I wanted to continue in the industries I was in. A lot of people didn't go back to their endeavors. And then I slowly started picking myself up again. Then I came here, and I realized that I did want to continue what I was doing. I don't think people will take enough time to reflect on what's going on, and that's why sometimes people lose themselves. Living here afforded me the time and atmosphere to think.

I didn't even know what my unit was gonna look like. I saw pictures, and the wine garden mixers sold me.

L.A.

I know, right. Having owned furniture stores, I was really ashamed of myself thinking, how could I decorate when I only remembered the bathroom?

Kyle

Yes, that's what I was thinking as well. The bathroom was gonna be amazing. The shower, the huge shower. But that is how I knew I had fallen in love with something unexplainable. Nothing was opened, no restaurant, no pool. We had each other, and that's all we needed. Then stuff started opening. We got to experience everything for the first time together. Everything was magical. I'm guessing it's how people feel when they go to Disney World for the first time because this is like Disney.

L.A.

Everyone was sitting in the newly opened bar, our everyone consisted of five people and then ten people.

Kyle

It was crazy. The compassion that everyone had for everyone, whether a tenant or a worker, didn't matter. It was like, we know that we're all in this together. When it was time to move on and buy a house, it was really hard. Because I knew it was financially a good investment for us before everything skyrocketed, my house has gone up by $70,000. It was tough to leave. I almost felt like I was on my own deployment here in a good way. I thought I was set for my own journey. It's how we were treated when we got here. You don't feel like you're renters. We were treated well even as we were leaving. When I told Winnie I was looking to buy a house? She goes, you've helped pay my bills; invest in yourself. That's Winnie. She's a Goddess

L.A.

You know, they're creating another development.

Kyle

Are you going to upgrade and go to the next property?

L.A.

I have to see what the next level of their dreams will build.

Kyle

Maybe we'll rent out our house?

L.A.

Kyle, I'd love to see more of you again.

WINNIE SCHULMAN

Axum Hospitality
Management LLC
President/ Founder
Partner in or at
Schulman Properties

L.A. Walker

When Nevada Governor Sisolak ordered all non-essential businesses to close for 30 days beginning March 18th, what were your thoughts?

Winnie Schulman

Too many to share. There was no option but to shut down the business.

So now what are we doing? Who will we have to let go.? How do you tell loyal, hardworking employees we have to let you go? These were the most challenging words to say and one of the most problematic situations I've ever encountered. I knew our employees' fears, wondering how they would survive after being told to stay home for a month while we figured out what was happening with the virus. I knew they were legitimately concerned about how they would survive. How will they pay their mortgages or rent, and how long before returning to normal? We had no answers. The arrival of COVID-19 was life-shattering.

My initial thoughts were that we'd be on vacation for a month. No problem. We're going to open a new place, and it's okay, everything will be fine. So one month passed, and two months passed, then three months. People were dying and becoming very ill. At that 90-day point, I can't tell you how I felt; I was in the twilight zone and felt like I was in an unknown world. I kept thinking about employees that had two and three kids. How frightening and humbling.

L.A.

Let's go back. When and how was the vision for creating a resort-style community conceived?

Winnie

Our project was conceived in Italy before COVID. Bob said, why don't I bring it to everyday people. They work hard, and they can have vacation every day. I looked at him.

L.A.

Winnie, I'm trying to hold back my laughter because I can imagine how you looked at Bob.

Winnie

It was alright. Bob said we love Italy. If I build it, they will come to rent it because it will be something they have never seen before in Multi-family anywhere in the USA.

L.A.

Were you apprehensive?

Winnie

Yes, but once Bob sets his mind, he will build what his heart sees. So, that's when and how the concept was born.

L.A.

It sounds like money and success were not the project motivators.

Winnie

Bob's motivation was always creating a unique community and a daily refuge for residents. A resort with the finest amenities where residents could enjoy work, play, and have community. Opening a full-service restaurant with a bar was an added intentional feature giving residents a place to meet, relax and unwind at home.

L.A.

At what point were you challenged with the thought of abandoning the project?

Winnie

On April 20, 2022, the construction was in full gear during the lockdown while we were sitting at home waiting for guidance on approaching the virus from the Governor's office.

L.A.

Would you like to stop?

Winnie

No. I'll go on. I'll take a deep breath. My head was spinning with several thoughts at once. Who will live here now in this costly project, I thought? Rent is not cheap, and so many are not working. So now, who will walk into this leasing office to sign a lease? The months continued with a daily diet of restrictions. Despite the ongoing construction, we hosted a food and wine reception for potential residents every Friday night during the late summer. We took a faith walk for sure. Our planned restaurant was not open, so we had food catered. We spent thousands. No matter how much we spent, Bob was confident things would be fine.

It's September, and people are moving in. We haven't opened the restaurant yet, but we've got the permits. We finally opened the restaurant on September 20th, 2020. I've been through three months to protect Bob's health. I faced people every day and feared bringing COVID home to Bob, so I stayed in the guest house.

L.A.

You had to make some gut-wrenching decisions. What kept you from giving up?

Winnie

There were many tough decisions. After getting the restaurant open, adhering to the restrictions began wearing on us. Most of the furniture had to be spread out, and nothing looked like I had imagined.

Do I keep the restaurant open or close it? It was a very tough financial decision. The restaurant idea became COVID friendly and a much-needed amenity for prospects to move in. Plus, we had already advertised it on every website and newspaper. Bob never wanted to compromise the concept of resort living. Who would we trust?

L.A.

The reputation you've amassed building apartment communities is evident with your South Beach property tenants who now live here, stating they could hardly wait for your latest project to open.

Winnie

We opened the South Beach property, I believe, in 2015. We gratefully enjoy many good relationships with South Beach tenants.

L.A.

What's next?

Winnie

We broke ground on a 232-unit community with penthouse apartments. The new project is very modern, and the style is different, but the concept is the same. The restaurant, spa, and exercise facility are larger, with an incredible onsite restaurant. The new build will express fresh amenity ideas from lessons learned from our properties.

L.A.

When is the anticipated date of completion?

Winnie

14-16 months.

L.A.

When you thought COVID-19 ended, what did it feel like to be attacked by the Omicron variant?

Winnie

You're told you're okay, then boom. We decided to close it because more staff became infected with Omicron than the original virus. We knew to return to normalcy, we needed to sanitize the kitchen and the entire premises. Sanitizing was once an easy process; we'd call, and a technician would come out and complete the task in hours. It took us three days to get someone out to sanitize because everyone was reopening, their business was booming everyone was hiring them. We closed for three days. We reopened for evening hours so residents could relax upon arriving home. Every decision we made focused on earning and maintaining resident and community trust; we worked hard so the answer would always be yes.

L.A

We've talked about restaurant staff and operations; how did your leasing staff manage all of the scheduling changes, mask mandates, and closures?

Winnie

Gabby! It's funny how Bob knew seven years ahead that Gabby had to be on our team. He met Gabby a long time ago, and he was so impressed with her knowledge of the product she was showing him and her elegance that is when he decided that Gabby would be the best to manage Tuscan Highlands. Gabby was the mother hen who guided the leasing staff through the COVID storm.

L.A.

We rarely see a woman in your capacity. Please share your journey to becoming a respected woman of color in a male-dominated industry.

Winnie

We don't see enough women of color in ownership and corporate partnership positions. Years ago, I would wear a name badge while attending all-male board meetings with Bob, and no one called me by my name. I was referred to as Bob's wife for almost two years. A board member asked me why I was there, and he suggested I spend my time at a spa instead. I shared my dilemma with my husband, he told me to find the words to address the issue, and he would support me 1000%. I sent out an email not to address me as Bob's wife when I sit in a meeting or any business setup. I took a stand, and Bob gave me his promised support. Let's say everyone now knows I'm a partner. I should not be defined by what they think, but by what I see in myself, I'm so proud of who I am, and I'm very comfortable in my skin. Bob and I have been intentional about having a diverse and inclusive staff.

L.A.

What do you want people to know about you?

Winnie

I'm a mother and grandmother, business owner, and wife who feels blessed to be supported by an amazing husband and great team.

L.A. WALKER

Executive Director
Social Issues
Theatre Author/Social
Writer/Playwright
President OPA Media
LLCEntrepreneur

By October 2019, My spouse had struggled with Lewy Body Dementia for over five years. We anchored in a senior living facility. While a premature living arrangement for me, the facility's safety, exercise, recreation, daily meals, and fellowshipping seemed the best alternative for us both.

The January 2020 announcement of the arrival of COVID-19 caused quite a mix of fear and uncertainty for senior living staff and residents. The months followed were full of regulations and restrictions, and residents were locked in, and visitors were locked out. The tone was dismal, frightening, and joyless.

Our thirty years together ended on June 24th, 2020. The presence of COVID-19 robbed me of an opportunity to hold a traditional funeral service. On July 18th, struggling to honor her life, I put together an online service with the help of friends. My long-time techie friend, Russ White of QVegas.com, had shared time with my spouse and me just months before her passing. He knew the depth of our love, and my tech skills came from a rotary phone. He offered to help me get the Celebration of Life service online.

I was adjusting to the absence of my spouse, and having no power to decide when to enter and exit a building, I became depressed. No, I mean depressed like I don't care anymore depressed. Three friends played online Scrabble with me every hour for over thirty days, determined to save me from being handcuffed to depression.

Russ White messaged me in August and told me of the new apartment development. He invited me to join him for the developer's hosted tour with complimentary wine and cocktails on any Friday night. I did. It took a couple of Friday night visits before I surrendered my fears and exchanged them for a new beginning. Part of the delay may have been not wanting the great food and wine gatherings to end, and they didn't. Those events introduced what my life as a resident would become. Becca's Restaurant and Lounge was not open when I moved into my new apartment on September 15th, 2020, but the grills and cabanas were. Russ and his business partner Garrett Pattiani decided to give me a COVID correct outdoor birthday party in late September. A beautifully diverse group of friends came masked and ready to eat, drink, and laugh. Friends I hadn't seen in months came, brought presents, and plenty of love. They were in awe of my new surroundings and excited to be together.

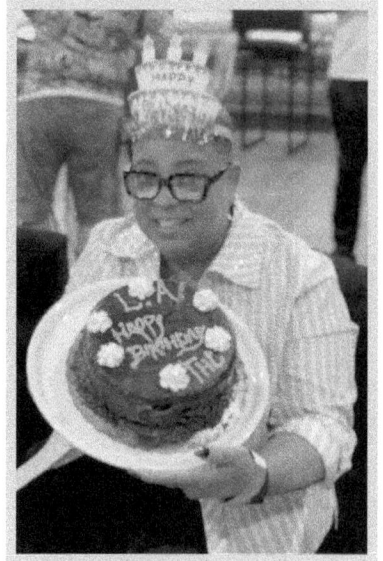

Becca's opened, and a small group of five gathered at the bar every evening. Our evening gathering grew to ten residents, then twenty, before reaching 200. Being an introvert-extrovert, the slow pace of meeting new residents as they moved in was perfect. There was a tone of sincere gratitude to have a place to exchange stories without judgment or reprisal. It was the first time I let down all the walls that hid my innermost feelings and concerns. I engaged with diverse and inclusive groups of people who sought commonness over exclusion. We didn't have any racially or politically charged conversations-none with undertones of unacceptance.

In contrast, the world struggled to share time while we were blessed to enjoy our days and evenings in a beautifully decorated safe space with fabulous people. We didn't need to leave the property, and the amenities provided opportunities to exercise, play indoor games, outdoor games, fire pits, lush landscaping, and food and drink.

As I have trekked a few miles around the clock, I can say without contradiction that this is one of the best living experiences I have ever had. It quite possibly saved my life.

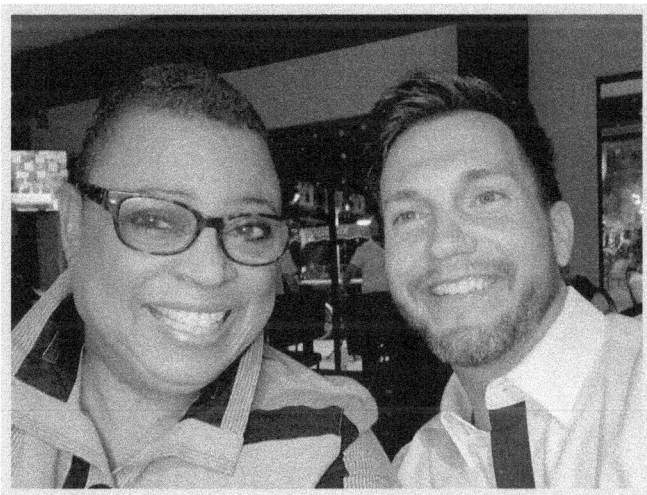

GARRETT PATTIANI

Co-Owner
QLife Media
Publisher QVegas
Magazine Owner
Bright Light
Holiday Company

In 2020, I was living in an awful apartment complex. There was heavy tension between all the residents and management. The property had failed to keep our building secure from the heavily populated homeless community and a very crime-heavy neighborhood. As a result of the pandemic, my husband and I had to confine ourselves to our apartment. He is a person that has a very disciplined routine and was starting the beginning of his life. It wasn't easy for him when his dreams, goals, and gym time were all taken away. I was trying to remain optimistic, but it was all getting to me.

I needed a change because I was worried that if something didn't give, I would have spiraled so far down that I might not be able to recover. I saw an ad for a new apartment complex outside the city that offered amenities that would be a dream in a global shutdown. As the layout and construction of certain parts of the complex might change, I figured that I would take a tour.

The tour was even better than what I saw not the website. The staff was friendly, and it offered the perfect oasis to relax, be entertained, and work. It was so lovely. It was such a lavish escape from what was happening in the rest of the world that a huge part of me felt a little guilty for being able to obtain such a gift. The other part of me knew that if I could be in a place that allowed me to be strong and confident, I would be able to help others get through this challenging time.

My husband and I decided to go separate, and this would be the first time in my life that I would be living alone, besides with my dog Dallas. I figured this would be a new start in paradise. I've celebrated holidays and birthdays and made friends for life. So far, this has been one of the most outstanding chapters of my life.

MARGARET KUYKENDALL

Entrepreneur

It's The Community For Me

Webster's dictionary defines community; as a group of people who live in the same area, such as a city, town, or neighborhood. But what is community really, and more importantly, how does it affect our daily lives for the better? I've been big on the whole "it takes a village" thing for as long as I can remember. My children always had grandparents, family, and friends who lived close by and did just about everything together daily. When my husband retired from the military, our daughter headed to college, and our son started middle school. We decided, like many Californians, to downsize and relocate to Las Vegas, NV. There were lots of pros... the cost of living was significantly less, and geographically it was still close to both northern and southern California. The one looming con was community since we didn't know anyone in Las Vegas. We decided to shrug off the doubt and headed to Las Vegas.

We settled on a newly developed full-time resort living community. It was packed full of on-site amenities like a football/soccer field, indoor-outdoor gym, dance studio, spa, sauna, jacuzzi, heated saltwater pool, sand volleyball court, herb garden, fire pits, outdoor kitchens, spa treatment rooms, dog parks, and a hair/nail Salon.

However, regardless of the on-site amenities, I was most looking forward to the slew of planned community events. Within less than a month of moving, it seemed as though we knew just about all our neighbors. Our direct community now includes people from almost every walk of life. Young families, college/grad students attend UNLV, active duty/retired military, business executives, small business owners, medical professionals, adult entertainers, professional sports athletes, and CA tech transplants. No matter their gender, nationality, sexual preference, pronouns, religion, political affiliation, or current relationship status, the common denominator seemed to be the same: a genuine desire to be part of an active community.

When the same developers built their second resort community about 20 minutes away, several residents put their names on the waitlist and reserved a spot site unseen. During the construction process, we were able to take pictures of our units being built from timber frame, to ribbon cutting. Four years and two developments later, our Las Vegas community is stronger than ever. Sure, people will come and go. There have been drama and magical once-in-a-lifetime moments alike. We have shared birthdays, anniversaries, and heartbreaking losses of life. Yet, when many of the world felt isolated and more alone than ever, our community road it out together for better or worse. The community is a living, ever-evolving, diverse group of people that hopefully grow together. It's perfectly imperfect, and I'm proud to be a part of just that.

:OMMUNITY UNITY

:ommunity is a tool we can utilize to main-
in our balance during uncertainty. When
e feel comfortable exchanging our chal-
nges, crying, and laughing together, we feel
cure. Community is a weapon of choice in
e preservation of mental wellness.

:eling hugged, supported, and included
iring times of distress keeps us sane.

:ommunity begins with inclusion, and
:lusion starts with us.

/e have work to do.

L.A. Walker is the Executive Director of
Social Issues Theatre (S.I.T.), author, and
playwright is a native Chicagoan who has
lived in Las Vegas for almost twenty years.

L.A. graduated from the U.S. Defense
Information School as a Radio and Television Broadcast Journalist. She became
a television anchor for the Southern
Command Network in Panama C.Z., then
a Baltimore radio news director.

In 2014 she brought her first play, *"Six No
Uptown,"* to the stage. A story inspired by
the art of her friend and mentor, the late
artist Annie F. Lee. Her other works include
"No Labels," the story of a homophobic dog
who gets adopted by a gay couple and freaks
out. *Ten Minutes of Truth on Racism, Jesus is
Mine,* her memoir *The Art of Seeing Beyond
the Mess,* and her latest body of work, The
COVID and Community series recognize
individuals and organizations whose efforts
brought light to dark times. All of her works
reflect her passion for social justice and
community education.

www.ingramcontent.com/pod-product-compliance
Lightning Source LLC
Chambersburg PA
CBHW022132280326
41933CB00007B/650